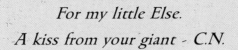

For my little Else.
A kiss from your giant - C.N.

Text copyright © 2004 Carl Norac
Illustrations copyright © 2004 Ingrid Godon
Moral rights asserted
Dual language copyright © 2004 Mantra Lingua
All rights reserved
A CIP record for this book is available
from the British Library.

First published in 2004 by Macmillan Children's Books, London
First dual language publication in 2004 by Mantra Lingua

mantra
5 Alexandra Grove, London N12 8NU
www.mantralingua.com

CARL NORAC

INGRID GODON

ぼくの　パパは　きょじんです

My Daddy is a Giant

Japanese translation by Mami Ozaki-Webster

mantra

ぼくの　パパは　きょじんです。
パパを　だきしめたいとき、
ぼくは　はしごに　のぼらなければ
なりません。

My daddy is a giant.
When I want to cuddle him,
I have to climb a ladder.

かくれんぼを　するとき、
パパは　やまの　うしろに
かくれます。

When we play hide-and-seek,
my daddy has to hide
behind a mountain.

そして、くもたちは
つかれたときに
ぼくの　パパの　かたに
のって　やすみます。

And when the clouds are tired,
they come and sleep
on my daddy's shoulders.

パパの　くしゃみは、
ハリケーンの　ようです。
うみも　ふきとばして　しまいます。

When my daddy sneezes,
it's like a hurricane.
It blows the sea away.

パパが　わらうと、
それもまた　ハリケーンの　ようです。
きから　はっぱが　ふきとびます。

When my daddy laughs,
it's like another hurricane.
All the leaves fly off the trees.

とりたちも　ぼくの　パパが
だいすきです。
パパの　あたまに　すを
つくります。

Birds love my daddy.
They make their nests
in his hair.

サッカーをするとき、
ぼくの　パパは　いつも　かちます。
パパは　つきに　とどくくらい
ボールを　けることが　できます。

When we play football,
my daddy always wins.

He can kick the ball as high as the moon.

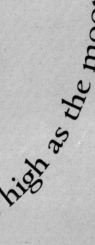

でも、ビーだまあそび　では　ぼくが
いつも　かちます。
パパの　ゆびは　おおきすぎるから。

But I always beat
him at marbles.
His fingers are
far too big.

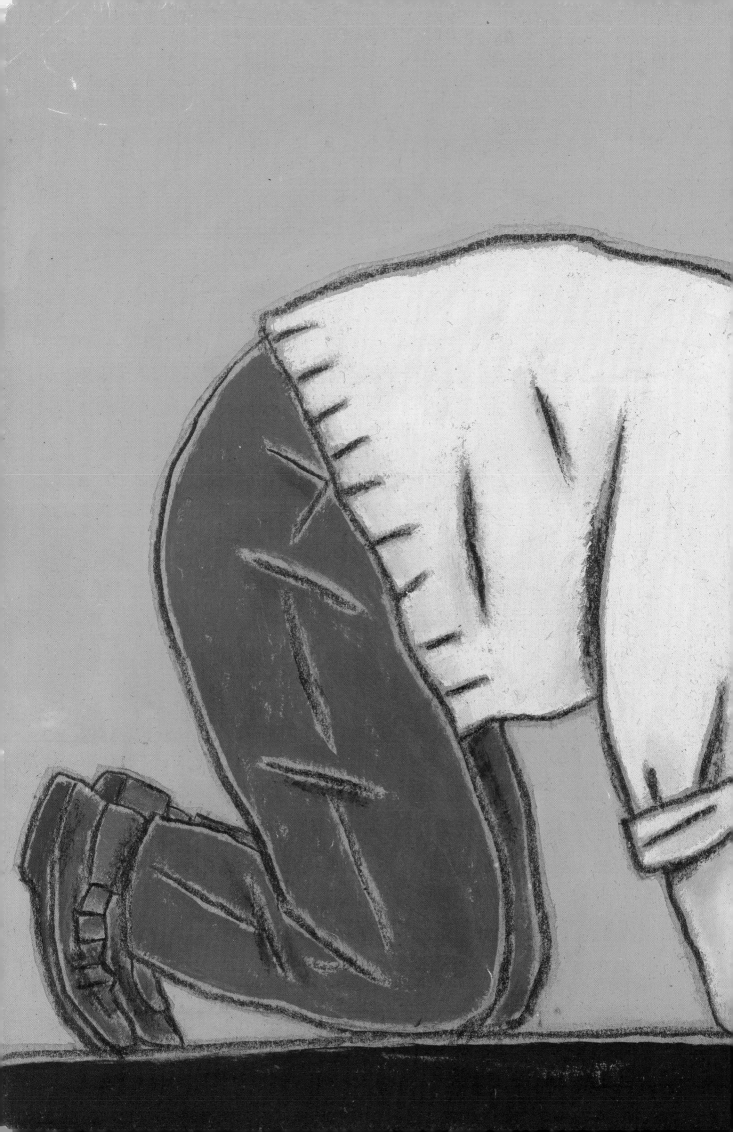

ぼくは　パパが　こんなふうに
いうのが　すきです。
「おまえは　パパみたいに
せが　たかくなってきたな。」って。

I like it when my
daddy says,
"You're getting as
tall as me!"

パパが　はしると、
まるで　こわがっているように
じめんが　ふるえます。

When my daddy runs,

the ground shakes

as if it was scared.

でも、パパの　うでの　なかに　いると、
ぼくは　なにも　こわくありません。

But I'm not scared
of anything when
I'm in my daddy's arms.

ぼくの　パパは　きょじんです。
そして、ぼくの　パパは　おおきなハートで
ぼくを　あいしてくれます。

My daddy is a giant,
and he loves me with
all his giant heart.